Turkish Delights

traditional music and dance

Rita Faelli

Australian Multicultural Foundation

Blake EDUCATION
Better ways to learn

Acknowledgments

We would like to thank the following for their assistance: Mr Cernal Akdenizr, Moreland Turkish Education and Social Welfare Centre; Ms Hilkat Ozgun, Australian Turkish Cultural Platform.

Turkish Delights: traditional music and dance
ISBN: 1 74164 110 1

Written by Rita Faelli
Copyright © 2006 Blake Publishing
Published by Blake Education Pty Ltd
ABN 50 074 266 023
108 Main Rd
Clayton South VIC 3168
Ph: (03) 9558 4433
Fax: (03) 9558 5433
email: mail@blake.com.au
Visit our website: www.blake.com.au

Harmony and Understanding program developed by UC Publishing Pty Ltd
Designers: Luke Sharrock and Cat Macinnes
Series Editor: Hass Dellal
Editor: Kerry Nagle

Printed in Malaysia by Thumbprints Utd Sdn Bhd

This publication is © copyright. No part of this book may be reproduced by any means without written permission from the publisher.

Photo and illustration credits:
MAPgraphics, page 6; Australian Turkish Cultural Platform, pages 8, 16, 17, 18, 19, 20, 22, 23, 24, 26, 27, 28; Jean Saint Martin, page 29.
All other photographs and illustrations are © copyright UC Publishing Pty Ltd.
Every effort has been made to trace the holders of copyrighted photographs. If any omission can be rectified, the publishers will be pleased to make the necessary arrangements.

Contents

Introduction 5

Our community school 7

Folk dances 8

Traditional costumes 10

Folktales............................... 12

Festival time 16

Dancing displays 18

Festival music 20

The mehter band.................... 22

Turkish delights 24

Jewellery............................. 26

Turkish carpets 28

Sharing cultures 30

Glossary 31

Index................................. 32

In this book ...

Introduction

Merhaba. My parents came from Turkey to live in this country. Even though I was not born in Turkey, my family still likes me to learn about Turkish culture and traditions.

At the weekend, I go to a Turkish community school to learn about our heritage. I really enjoy attending special events that celebrate Turkish culture, like the Tulip Festival.

Word fact
Merhaba means hello in Turkish.

Country facts: Turkey

- Turkey lies between Europe and Asia. Part of Turkey, called Thrace, is in Europe and the larger part, called Anatolia, is in Asia.
- Turkey has a population of about 68 million people.
- The capital is Ankara and the largest city is Istanbul.
- The main religion of Turkey is Islam.
- Turkish is the sixth most widely-spoken language in the world.
- Many great civilisations began in Turkey. Turkey was the centre of two of the major empires in history – the Byzantine and the Ottoman Empires.

Our community school

At our community school, we learn the Turkish language, folk dances and music.

One day I want to visit Turkey and speak with my relatives in Turkish. The language is difficult, but I am getting better.

Fast fact
In Turkey today, folk dances and folk songs are so important that they are considered cultural treasures. They are important because they keep traditions alive.

Folk dances

It's fun learning about Turkish folk dances and performing them.

Some folk dances are hundreds of years old. The dances are special because they reflect the customs and the history of the region.

Some dances describe everyday chores, like baking bread or working in the fields. Some dances are about the harvest. There are special dances for occasions like weddings, or religious and national festivals.

There are thousands of different folk dances throughout Turkey. There's no way we could ever learn them all. We're happy to know just a few of them.

Our teachers take us through the dance steps very slowly. They explain what each movement means.

The dances usually start slowly and then get faster. You can feel the drums and the other instruments pick up the beat and it makes us want to race along with them.

Traditional costumes

When we perform, we are allowed to wear traditional costumes. These costumes are usually made from layers of different, brightly-coloured fabrics.

Turkish costumes, like Turkish folk dances, change from region to region. There are hundreds of different styles of traditional clothing for both men and women.

For some dances, the girls wear a headdress. It can be plain or decorated with jewellery or other ornaments.

Fast fact
Turkish costumes are usually made from locally woven fabrics. Turkey is famous for its fine weaving and embroidery.

Folktales

Traditional Turkish folktales are great fun to listen to. Many folktales also have folk songs in them.

At first I thought they sounded very strange. Now I know that Turkish folktales are very old. The stories have been passed down through generations.

Fairytales

Fairytales in English usually begin with "Once upon a time". Turkish folktales have special beginnings, too. Here are some common ones.

- A long, long, time ago, when the sieve was inside the straw, when the donkey was the town crier and the camel was the barber …
- Once there was; once there wasn't.
- Once, when God's creatures were as plentiful as grains and talking too much was a sin …

Here is a story about a girl who was very lazy. There is also a folk song in it.

The lazy girl and the beggar

Once upon a time, when the fleas were barbers, the camels were town criers, and I was rocking my mother's cradle, there was a wife and husband.

The wife and husband had a daughter. She had been brought up very carefully but she didn't learn any housework. Because of this, she was called the Lazy Girl.

Her parents would say to their daughter, "Get up, girl, and *do* something."

"I can't be bothered," the Lazy Girl would reply.

When she grew up, her parents arranged for the Lazy Girl to marry a hunter. "You'll have to get up and do something now that you are married," said the parents. But the girl didn't change a bit. She just kept on being lazy.

One day, her husband went hunting. "There is a duck roasting in the oven for supper," said the hunter. "Take care to watch the fire."

"Yeah, yeah," mumbled the Lazy Girl. But she didn't bother to check on the roasting duck.

After a while, a beggar came by the house. "Please, lady, can you spare a bit of bread?" cried the beggar.

"You can get it yourself. It's in the kitchen," answered the Lazy Girl, not bothering to move.

So the beggar went to the kitchen. He saw the duck in the oven. "Oh, this smells delicious. I think I'll take the duck and put it in my bag. I'll put my old, smelly shoes in the oven. That girl is so lazy she won't know the difference," said the beggar. He went back to the Lazy Girl and said, "I found the bread, lady. Let me sing a song to thank you for your kindness." And he sang,

Your duck is in my bag,
My shoes are in your pan.
You lie in your bed,
While I eat your duck in the forest.

By the time the Lazy Girl realised what had happened, the beggar had gone.

When her husband came home and found his dinner was gone, he was cross. "Because of your laziness, you were fooled by a simple beggar. Now, we have no supper."

And as she went to bed hungry, the Lazy Girl vowed she would never be lazy again – and she never was!

Festival time

Festivals are a great time to enjoy yourself. There are displays, music, dancing, food and a chance to share our traditions with people of our new home.

The Tulip Festival is a traditional festival that celebrates the Turkish origins of the tulip.

Tulips

- Tulips are native to Central Asia and Turkey.

- Tulips were first brought to the Netherlands in the 16th century. The Dutch are now famous for their production of tulips.

- In Turkey, the period between 1718–1730 is called the Tulip Era. Tulips of all kinds were very popular. It was common for embroidery, textiles, clothing, carpets, tiles and paintings to have tulip designs or shapes.

- The word "tulip" comes from the Turkish word for turban, *tulbend*, which it resembles in shape.

- The tulip is a symbol of Turkey.

Dancing displays

The festival is a great opportunity to see Turkish dance groups perform.

This year, we saw a group dance the *horon*, a dance from the Black Sea region. In Turkey, each village has its own variation of the horon. It is danced at traditional celebrations like weddings and harvests.

Fast fact
Horon comes from the word *horom* which refers to a line of corn stalks tied together to form a lattice. From a distance, the lattice looks like a line of people joining hands with their arms raised.

Another group performed a dance from the north-eastern part of Turkey. The dance, called the *kafkas*, is a very old form of traditional dancing in Turkey.

This dance is performed by both boys and girls. In this dance, the boys are trying to win the hearts of the girls.

19

Festival music

At the festival, Turkish musicians bring the crowds to life with their music.

Turkish folk music is very lively and vibrant. The folk songs tell stories about work, daily life, love, or they can just be great to dance to!

Not all the music at the festival is traditional. One group performs a blend of traditional and original Turkish songs mixed with reggae, funk and dancehall. A belly dancer performs to their music.

Fast facts

- Traditional instruments are still popular in Turkey and are sometimes played at weddings and other celebrations.

- The most commonly-used, stringed, folk instrument in Turkey is called a *saz*. It is a type of long-necked lute. Traditionally, a saz was played only by a travelling musician.

- Other popular folk instruments are the *zurna* and *davul*. The zurna is a woodwind instrument and the davul is a bass drum.

The mehter band

One of the most exciting musical performances you can hear at the festival is by the mehter band.

Mehter bands are primarily military bands. They were first formed in the 13th century to march into battle with the Ottoman army. The powerful sounds of the music gave the Ottoman soldiers strength and courage.

> **Fast fact**
> Many elements of mehter music influenced western composers, particularly in the 17th century. A striking example of this is the use of Turkish drums in Beethoven's *Ninth Symphony*.

There is a variety of instruments in the mehter band, including:

- çevgâns (jingling instruments in the form of a crescent)
- zurnas (woodwind)
- trumpets
- small kettledrums
- cymbals
- bass drums
- kös drums (giant kettledrums).

> **Fast fact**
> In the past, some kös drums were over one metre in height. They were carried on camels while the rest of the band marched.

23

Turkish delights

One of the best parts to Turkish festivals is food. There are always many stalls selling sweet and savoury Turkish specialties.

Gözleme is a dish made of flat bread. The bread is folded over various fillings and then baked on a griddle. It has been a popular light meal for centuries in Turkey.

Popular fillings for gözleme are spinach, minced lamb, feta cheese and mashed potatoes.

Kebap (or kebab) means "roasted" and usually refers to lamb roasted in some form. The doner kebap is often called Turkey's national dish. It is lamb roasted on a vertical spit and sliced off when done.

Delicious, crisp, honeyed doughnuts called *lokma* are popular at the festival. These treats are made for special occasions.

Jewellery

As well as food, dancing and music, there are plenty of craft displays. Jewellery stalls are very popular.

Turkish jewellery is ornate and colourful. Some of the styles that are worn today have been popular for centuries.

Traditionally, jewellery was not just decorative. It was important for its value. The more jewellery a woman owned, the higher her position in the community. Jewellery could be converted to cash if you needed money.

Word fact
The word "turquoise" comes from a word meaning "Turkish". It was derived from the beautiful colour of the Mediterranean Sea on the southern Turkish coast.

A special charm

- Charms that protect against the "evil eye" are a popular type of jewellery. These charms are called nazar bonjuk.

- For thousands of years, Turkish artisans have created blue glass "eyes". These are meant to look straight back at anyone who casts a spell on the wearer. It's as if the blue eye is saying, "I see what you're doing, and you can't get away with it!"

- Nazar bonjuk evil eye charms are hand crafted of blown glass in Turkey and come in many shapes and sizes.

- These charms are worn all over Turkey. Women use them as bracelets, earrings or necklaces.

Turkish carpets

Turkish carpets are on display at nearly all Turkish festivals. Carpets made in Turkey are exported all over the world.

Carpet weaving has a long tradition in Turkey. The designs, colours, and quality of the carpets are so unique that the region and village where the carpets were made can be identified.

In Turkey, carpets have three main functions: religious, artistic and as domestic home furnishing.

Carpets have been woven for family use by village women for centuries.

Fast fact

In the past, a woman had a greater chance of getting married if she was a skilled weaver. She would offer carpets as part of her dowry to her future husband. She would take great care with the dyeing and hand-spinning of the wool, and with selecting designs.

Sharing cultures

We love learning about traditional Turkish culture. We also like to share these things with people who are not familiar with our music, dance and craft.

Turkish festivals are great because lots of people from different backgrounds join in and have fun. I think that's the best way for people to understand each other.

Glossary

artisans — people who do skilled work, making things with their hands

calligraphy — beautiful writing using special pens or brushes

cultural — belonging to the beliefs, ways of life, art and customs shared by people in a particular society

dowry — the property or money given by a woman to a man when they marry

embroidery — a pattern sewn onto cloth

folklore — the traditional stories and customs of a particular area or country

griddle — a round iron plate that is used for cooking on top of a stove

heritage — the traditional beliefs, values and customs of a family, country or society

legends — old, well-known stories, often about brave people, adventures or magical events

myths — ideas or stories which many people believe, but which are not true

town crier — someone employed in the past to walk around the streets of a town, shouting news, warnings, etc.

Index

community school   5, 7

costumes   7, 10, 11

crafts   7, 16, 26, 27, 28, 29

folk dances   7, 8, 9, 10, 18, 19, 20

folktales   12, 13, 14, 15

food   8, 24, 25

music   7, 20, 21, 22, 23

Tulip Festival   16, 18, 19, 20, 22, 24, 25, 26, 27, 28, 30

tulips   16, 17

Turkey   5, 6, 7, 9, 17, 18, 19, 21, 24, 25, 27, 28, 29